Georgie Woolridge

Birds

A Mindful Coloring Book

St. Martin's Griffin
New York

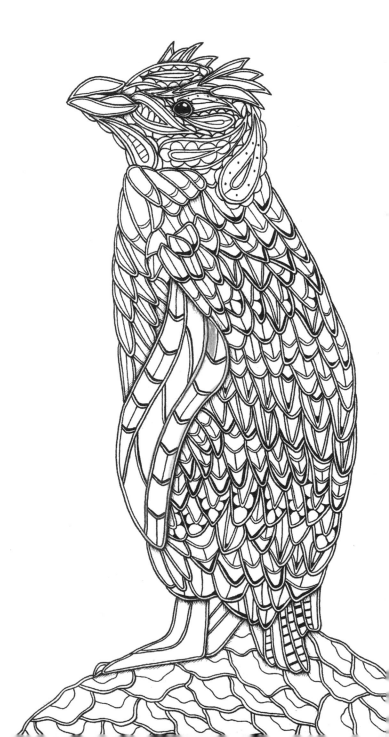

INTRODUCTION

Birds are one of the biggest inspirations for my art to date, and it has been a pleasure to choose the species that we have included in this book. The wide variety of colors and shapes are fascinating, and they are so interesting to draw. From the tall and leggy ostrich to the tiny tailorbird, each bird has a special appeal and a personality all its own.

Each drawing is accompanied by a short description that will give you some tips on the bird's real colors, but part of the fun of this book is that you can let your imagination take over and choose any colors you want! Art has no boundaries, do it your way!

The hummingbird is probably my favorite bird, and it was the very first one I drew. I found that in creating the texture for the bird's feathers I could incorporate the swirling paisley patterns that I had come to adore while traveling in India. I loved the results so much that I immediately began to experiment with other birds. I also drew on my

travels to Thailand, Vietnam, Singapore, Australia, and New Zealand, picking out local styles and choosing birds that I had seen in the wild and I felt possessed a unique charm and character.

There's also something about the freedom of birds that I really love—the fact that they can escape and soar above the world —it's the same feeling that I get when I draw and I really hope you will find the same sort of pleasure when you color them.

As our lives become increasingly burdened by over-stimulation and technological burnout,

drawing, coloring, and other art techniques are becoming a lifeline for stressed-out and busy people of all ages. By taking time out to concentrate on the simple practice of creating a beautifully colored image, the mind is distanced from the usual pressures of life and able to focus on the space and time it occupies in that present moment. Easing you out of your everyday worries and into another world that is all your own.

When it comes to coloring my designs, I like to use a variety of ProMarker pens and touches of watercolor. I also love to blend different mediums together to create beautiful effects. Sometimes the vividness

of pen over the subtle colors of crayons, pencils, chalks, and pastels really adds to the final outcome—but you can use any methods you want. I would recommend trying out pastels and chalks for the larger areas of pattern, and crayons and pencils for the smaller details. Or any mixture of all these could also make really beautiful pieces of art. It's all up to you!

Otherwise, my only piece of advice is that you have fun with these birds and color them as suits you. I really hope you enjoy coloring them as much as I enjoyed creating them.

Georgie Woolridge

MANDARIN DUCK

('mændərɪn dʌk,' *Aix galericulata*)

Although native to East Asia, the mandarin duck has established a sizable population in other countries as a result of escapes from captivity. Adult male mandarin ducks have an elaborate and ornate plumage with long orange feathers on the side of the face, orange "sails" on the back, a purple breast, and pale orange flanks. They are usually between 16 to 19 in (41–49 cm) in length.

BARN OWL
('bɑːn aʊl,' *Tyto alba*)

The barn owl, with its heart-shaped face, buff back and wings, and pure white underside, is a familiar countryside bird. A typical barn owl measures around 13 to 15 in (33–39 cm) in overall length. It is the most widespread land bird species in the world and found on every continent except Antarctica.

FLAMINGO
('fləˈmɪŋɡəʊ,' *Phoenicopterus*)

Long-legged flamingos are recognized all over the world, but the large species of American flamingo native to Florida is undoubtedly the best known. Adult birds are around 3 ft (100 cm) tall and their famous brightly colored plumage can be pink, orange, or white depending on their diet. The algae and crustaceans that they eat contain pigments called carotenoids that color their feathers.

HUMMINGBIRD

('hʌmɪŋbɜːd,' *Trochilidae*)

There are more than 300 species of hummingbird, many of which are distinguished by the colorful plumage on their wings and throats. These tiny birds—they are usually around 3 in (8 cm) in length—are native to the Americas and prefer wooded and forested areas with plenty of flowers, although some have been recorded living in deserts, coastal regions, and meadows.

ROCKHOPPER PENGUIN

('rɒkhɒpə pɛŋgwɪn,' *Eudyptes chrysocome*)

The rockhopper is a small species of penguin, standing at an average of 22 in (55 cm) when fully grown. The males and females look so similar that only DNA tests can tell them apart. The rockhopper penguin got its name from the hopping motion it uses to get around its habitat on the craggy islands north of Antarctica. Year after year they return to the same breeding ground to mate.

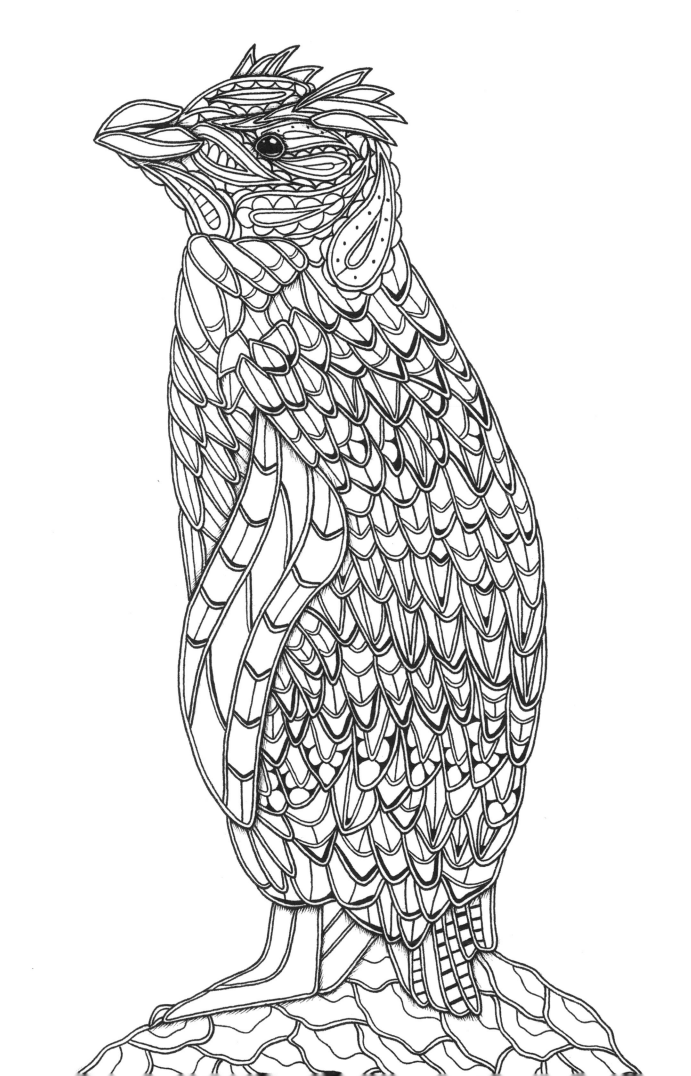

COMMON TAILORBIRD

('kɒmən teɪləbəːd,' *Orthotomus sutorius*)

The common tailorbird is a small songbird—around 4¾ in (12 cm) in length —found throughout tropical Asia. The bird's name comes from their method of sewing together leaves with plant fibers, or even spider silk, to create a cradle into which they build their nests. The common tailorbird is very comfortable with humans and is quickly colonizing urban areas.

BLACK KITE
('blak kʌɪt,' *Milvus migrans*)

Black kites like to soar and glide on thermals as they hunt, using their amazing sense of vision to search for food. The birds feed on lizards, fish, small mammals, and insects. They are identified by their angled wings—which have an average span of 57 in (145 cm)—and distinctive tail feathers. Kites are found across the Australian mainland, as well as in Africa, Asia, and Europe.

INDIAN ROLLER

('ɪndɪən rəʊlə,' *Coracias benghalensis*)

The Indian roller is common across tropical Asia, with its territory stretching from Iraq to Indochina. The bird's stunning acrobatic aerial twists and turns give the roller its name. They prefer grassland and scrub habitats, and are often seen perched in trees and on wires along roadsides. These decorative birds are about 10 in (25 cm) long, and a captivating mix of blue, green, ocher, and lilac.

HOOPOE
('huːpuː,' *Upupa epops*)

The hoopoe is exotic in its appearance as well as its name, which derives from the distinctive sound of the bird's call. Widespread in Europe, Asia, and Africa, hoopoes have even been spotted flying at high-altitudes across the Himalayas. They are around 5 in (12 cm) in length and sport an impressive orange "crown."

LAUGHING DOVE
('lɑːfɪŋ dʌv,' *Spilopelia senegalensis*)

This small species of pigeon is so named because of its characteristic call, that sounds a little like human laughter. The birds are found in sub-Saharan Africa, the Middle East, and the Indian subcontinent and prefer scrubland and desertlike habitats. They are usually 9¾ in (25 cm) in length with pinkish feathers on their undersides and lilac coloring around their head and neck.

RHODE ISLAND RED CHICKEN
('rəʊd ʌɪlənd rɛd tʃɪkɪn,' *Gallus gallus domesticus*)

This handsome breed of American domestic chicken has rich, rust-colored feathers, a red-brown beak, and yellow legs. Rhode Island Reds grow to an average of 10–15¾ in (25–40 cm) in length and are reliable layers, which contributes to their popularity with backyard chicken keepers. In 1954 the breed, as its name suggests, was designated the state bird of Rhode Island.

LITTLE CORMORANT
('lɪt(ə)l kɔːm(ə)r(ə)nt,' *Microcarbo niger*)

The little cormorant is widely found across the Indian subcontinent and extends through to Java, where it is sometimes called the Javanese cormorant. The little cormorant is about 20 in (50 cm) long and like all cormorants eats fish, catching its food by diving from the surface. The iconic pose of the cormorant with wings spread on a rock to dry was regularly used in European medieval heraldry.

RED-BREASTED GOOSE
(ʻrɛd brɛstɪd guːs,ʼ *Branta ruficollis*)

The red-breasted goose has a very distinct plumage of stark black and white feathers offset by a splendid rust-colored chest and is around 21½ in (55 cm) in length. The birds breed in Arctic Siberia, but travel to Bulgaria, Romania, and Ukraine in winter. However, escapees from captivity have ensured that the birds can be found more widely across Europe.

EUROPEAN ROBIN

('jʊərəˈpiːən rɒbɪn,' *Erithacus rubecula*)

Famous for its bright red breast, the robin is observed throughout the year in hedges and back yards across all of the United Kingdom. Despite their festive reputation, and repeatedly being voted the UK's favorite bird, robins are surprisingly aggressive and drive other birds away from their territory. They feed on worms, seeds, and insects and are usually around 5 in (13 cm) in length.

BLUE TIT

('bluː tɪt,' *Cyanistes caeruleus*)

The blue tit is a very popular and instantly recognizable visitor to yards throughout temperate Europe and western Asia. Their plumage is a brightly colored mix of blue, yellow, white, and green and the birds are well known for their bright blue caps. Blue tits are an average length of 4¾ in (12 cm) and enjoy a diet of insects, spiders, and seeds.

BAR-HEADED GOOSE
('bɑː hɛdɪd guːs,' *Anser indicus*)

This tough breed is identified by the black bands on their heads that give them their name. They are the world's highest-flying birds (rumor has it that they fly higher than Mount Everest when they migrate over the Himalayas) and have adapted to cope with low oxygen levels and low temperatures. These mid-sized geese are native to China and Russia and are around 29 in (74 cm) long.

EURASIAN TEAL
(ˈjʊ(ə)ˈreɪʃ(ə)n tiːl,' *Anas crecca*)

Male teals have reddish-brown heads with distinctive emerald green swatches around their eyes. The flanks are gray and tail-feathers are yellow with black edges. The females are a more discreet speckled brown. In winter the birds gather in the south and west of the United Kingdom, having traveled from the Baltic and Siberia. They are usually around 14 in (36 cm) in length.

BLUE-FOOTED BOOBY
('bluː fʊtɪd buːbi,' *Sula nebouxii*)

The blue-footed booby is easily recognized by its bright blue feet, which the males use to attract female partners in an elaborate mating dance that involves a lot of strutting and stamping. Measuring up to 36 in (90 cm) in length, females are generally slightly larger than males. The majority of birds nest on the Galápagos Islands, consuming a diet of fish caught when swimming underwater.

KOOKABURRA

(ˈkʊkəˌbʌrə,' *Dacelo*)

Kookaburras are a species of kingfisher found in Australia and New Guinea. The birds are around 13¾ in (35 cm) in length on average and sport vivid blue speckled wings and long sharp beaks. The name kookaburra echoes the bird's call, which has the quality of bubbling laughter. They are equally at home in forestland or the savanna, as well as wooded suburban areas.

RAINBOW BEE-EATER

('reɪnbəʊ biː iːtə,' *Merops ornatus*)

The rainbow bee-eater has a spectacular plumage of green, blue, and yellow; a curving bill; and long trailing tail-feathers. It has a golden crown and orange-yellow throat, separated from its green chest by a black band. Averaging 8 in (20 cm) in length, bee-eaters are native to wooded areas in mainland Australia, where they can be observed swooping and diving swiftly after flying insects.

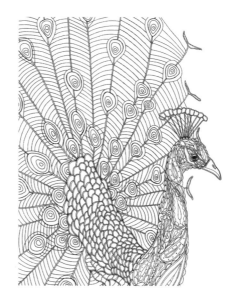

PEACOCK
('piːkɒk,' *Pavo*)

Peacocks are universally known for their vibrant blue and green tail feathers that make up their iconic mating display. Measuring from bill to tail peacocks can grow to 46 in (115 cm) in length. There are two species, the blue peacock from India and Sri Lanka and the green peacock native to Java and Burma. The blue peacock is also the national bird of India.

KINGFISHER
('kɪŋfɪʃə,' *Alcedines*)

Kingfishers are well known for their iridescent plumage, with bright orange chests and glowing blue wings dappled with violet and ultramarine tones. The birds are usually around 6 in (15 cm) in length, and can dive so fast that their long beaks can pierce ice. Their habitats are the lakes, ponds, and slow moving rivers of Europe, North Africa, and Asia.

AMERICAN GOLDFINCH
(ˈəˈmɛrɪk(ə)n ɡəʊl(d)fɪn(t)ʃ,ˈ *Spinus tristis*)

The American goldfinch is around 4¾ in (12 cm) in length. Their beaks are usually pink but become bright orange in the spring. The birds shed their feathers twice a year and in the spring the male birds become a vivid shade of cadmium yellow in order to attract a mate. The female birds remain brown, but wear a lighter yellow bib.

PINK-BACKED PELICAN

(ˈpɪŋk bakd pɛlɪk(ə)n,ˈ *Pelecanus rufescens*)

Although small for a pelican, the pink-backed pelican is still a sizable bird, measuring between 49 and 61 in (125–155 cm) in length. Its yellowy bill can be up to 15 in (38 cm) in itself. The bird's habitat is the swamps and lakes of Africa, the Arabian Peninsula, and southern India. Adults have long feathers on their heads and their plumage is a grayish pink that gives the species its name.

BLUE JAY
('bluː dʒeɪ,' *Cyanocitta cristata*)

Blue jays have, as their name suggests, a mostly pale blue plumage with a white chest, a distinctive bright blue crest, and a black collar at their necks. They are native to the eastern and central United States as well as southern Canada. Blue jays breed in woodlands, often near residential areas. Both the male and female birds have similar plumage, and are usually around 10¼ in (26 cm) in length.

TAWNY OWL

(''tɔːni aʊl,' *Strix aluco)*

The round head and face of the tawny (or brown) owl is surrounded by dark feathers. Its plumage is red-brown with paler colors on the body. These owls are frequently heard at night in rural areas, but only seen rarely. Like other owls, the birds hunt at night for rodents, guided by their exceptional sense of hearing. They can vary from 15 to 18 in (37–46 cm) in length.

OSTRICH

(ˈɒstrɪtʃ,' *Struthio camelus*)

The long legs of the ostrich can reach speeds of 43 mph (70 km/h), and can also administer a powerful kick to predators. With an average height of 8 ft (2.4 m) the ostrich is the largest of all birds and lays the largest eggs. They live in groups and, when under threat, try to conceal themselves by lying flat on the ground. The male birds have a striking black-and-white plumage, while the fluffy feathered females are a lighter brown.

DOMESTICATED TURKEY

('dəˈmɛstɪkeɪtɪd təːki,' *Meleagris gallopavo*)

Domesticated turkeys have a fine display of speckled bronze-brown and black plumage and on average grow to 39 in (100 cm) in length. Male turkeys are known as toms and the red flesh above the beak is called the snood, while on the underside hangs the wattle. The birds are native to the Americas and evidence suggests they were domesticated 2,000 years ago by indigenous peoples.

ROSE-RINGED PARAKEET
('afrɪk(ə)n rəʊz rɪŋd parəkiːt,' *Psittacula krameri*)

Male rose-ringed parakeets have a red or black ring around their necks
and the rest of their plumage is a beautiful, vivid bright green. They are around
16 in (40 cm) in length, a measurement that includes their long tail feathers.
The birds are also known for their loud squawks and are native to Guinea,
Senegal, Mauritania, Uganda, Sudan, and Egypt.

GOLDEN EAGLE

('gəʊld(ə)n iːg(ə)l,' *Aquila chrysaetos*)

Golden eagles are rare, yet they remain one of the most celebrated birds of prey. The birds can grow to 40 in (102 cm) in length, sometimes with a wingspan of 7 ft 8 in (2.34 m). They have dark brown plumage with their name stemming from the golden feathers on the back of their head and neck. Their agility and speed, along with their sharp talons, make them a formidable predator.

MAGPIE

('magpʌɪ,' *Pica pica*)

Magpies are considered the most intelligent bird species and are the only non-mammal to be able to recognize themselves in a mirror. Part of the crow family, magpies are widespread across Europe and Asia. Although historically seen as a bird of bad omen in European cultures, in China and Korea they are believed to bring good fortune. Magpie coloring is a mix of glossy black and pure white with blue-green detail on the wings, which generally span 20 to 24 in (51–61 cm).

GYRFALCON
('dʒəːˌfɔː(l)k(ə)n,' *Falco rusticolus*)

The largest falcon species, the gyrfalcon is the national symbol of Iceland, and has been highly valued by Norsemen for centuries as a precise and efficient hunter. It is found in Arctic regions and the islands of North America, Europe, and Asia. Its plumage can vary from all-white to dark brown depending on its location, but is often a vivid mix of speckles with a sharp yellow beak. The gyrfalcon has a powerful wingspan of 4 to 4½ feet (1.2–1.3 m).

GALAH

(ˈgəˈlɑ, *Eolophus roseicapilla*)

Also known as a rose-breasted cockatoo, the galah is a common Australian species that is found in open country and increasingly in built-up areas. They grow to about 14 in (35 cm) in length and have a pale gray back with a deep pink face and chest. They also have a pale pink mobile crest, which makes them instantly recognizable as being part of the cockatoo family.

GREATER ROADRUNNER

('greɪtər rəʊdrʌnə,' *Geococcyx californianus*)

The roadrunner is well-known in its cartoon incarnation, but the real bird is actually a member of the cuckoo family. They can grow to 2 ft (62 cm) in length and have a tufty crest atop their heads. Their plumage is dark brown with gold spots and white speckles, with hints of blue on the neck. Roadrunners have 4 toes on each foot, which allows them to run down their prey at speed.

PURPLE HERON

('pəːp(ə)l hɛr(ə)n,' *Ardea purpurea*)

The purple heron can grow to a height of 37 in (94 cm) and has a reddish-brown plumage, which becomes a darker gray across the back in adults, giving the effect of purple-mauvish tones. The heron also has darker stripes leading down from its head to the base of its long neck. They are native to Africa, central and southern Europe, and southern and eastern Asia.

LITTLE RINGED PLOVER
('lɪt(ə)l rɪŋd plʌvə,' *Charadrius dubius*)

These small birds—adults grow to an average 7 in (18 cm) in length—have striking black-and-white markings around their heads and necks. Their beaks are black and their little white bodies with buff-gray wings sit on top of pale yellowish legs. They breed near freshwater and river edges in Europe and western Asia, utilizing the stony ground and gravel pits to make their nests.

CALIFORNIA QUAIL
(ˈkalɪˈfɔːnɪə kweɪl,ʼ *Callipepla californica*)

The ground-dwelling California quail likes soft, freshly turned soil in which they can burrow down and use their bodies and wings to create dust baths. They are native to the United States and have been introduced across South America, South Africa, and Australia. Adults are 10 in (25 cm) in length and have a distinctive curving crest that droops forward. Males are more decorative, with a dark brown cap, a black face, gray-blue chest, and light brown underside.

American Goldfinch 48–49

Bar-Headed Goose 34–35

Barn Owl 6–7

Black Kite 16–17

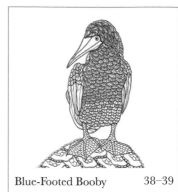

Blue-Footed Booby 38–39

Blue Jay 52–53

Blue Tit 32–33

California Quail 76–77

Common Tailorbird 14–15

Domesticated Turkey 58–59

Eurasian Teal 36–37

European Robin 30–31

Flamingo 8–9

Galah 68–69

Golden Eagle 62–63

Greater Roadrunner 70–71

Gyrfalcon 66–67

Hoopoe 20–21

Hummingbird 10–11

Indian Roller 18–19

Kingfisher 46–47

Kookaburra 40–41

Laughing Dove 22–23

Little Cormorant 26–27

Little Ringed Plover 74–75

Magpie 64–65

Mandarin Duck 4–5

Ostrich 56–57

Peacock 44–45

Pink-Backed Pelican 50–51

Purple Heron 72–73

Rainbow Bee-Eater 42–43

Red-Breasted Goose 28–29

Rhode Island Red 24–25

Rockhopper Penguin 12–13

Rose-Ringed Parakeet 60–61

Tawny Owl 54–55

Author's Acknowledgments

I would like to express appreciation to my family and friends for their support and encouragement throughout the designing of this book. I am excited to bring you my art and I really hope you enjoy it.

BIRDS.

Copyright © 2015 by Elwin Street Limited. All rights reserved.

For information, address St. Martin's Press, 175 Fifth Avenue, New York, N.Y. 10010.
www.stmartins.com

Conceived and produced by
Elwin Street Limited
3 Percy Street
London W1T 1DE
www.elwinstreet.com

Library of Congress Cataloging-in-Publication Data Available Upon Request

ISBN 978-1-250-09502-2

First U.S. Edition: October 2015

Our books may be purchased in bulk for promotional, educational, or business use. Please contact your local bookseller or the Macmillan Corporate and Premium Sales Department at (800) 221-7945, extension 5442, or by e-mail at MacmillanSpecialMarkets@macmillan.com.

10 9 8 7 6 5 4 3

Printed in Singapore